STUDY GUIDE ON THE HOLY SPIRIT

"FAITH COMES BY HEARING AND HEARING BY THE WORD OF GOD."

CHAPTER 1
INTRODUCTION TO THE HOLY SPIRIT

I. **The Trinity**

   A. There is one God manifested in three persons: the Father, the Son, and the Holy Spirit (1 Timothy 3:16).

   B. I think the term *triunity* more clearly indicates the "Three-in-One" aspect of the Godhead.

   C. In Hebrew, the singular word for *God* is "El", the dual tense is "Elah," and the word Elohim is used to indicate three or more. *Elohim* is the word translated "God" in Genesis 1:1.

II. **The Holy Spirit is a Person**

   A. The Holy Spirit is thought by some to be an "essence" or "power" of God rather than a separate person, because *ruach,* the Hebrew word for *Spirit,* also means "breath;" and "pneuma," the Greek word for *Spirit,* also means "wind" or "air." As Christians, we know He is a person.

   The early church scholar, Arias, caused division with his declaration that God the Father was the only true God, that Jesus was a created being, and the Holy Spirit was only an essence. This doctrine is known as the Arian heresy.

   B. The Holy Spirit has the characteristics of a person

   1. 1 Corinthians 2:10–11—The Holy Spirit searches and has knowledge.
   2. 1 Corinthians 12:11—The Holy Spirit distributes gifts as He wills.
   3. Romans 8:27—He has a mind.
   4. Romans 15:30—He loves us.

5. He testifies of Jesus and exalts the Father and Son over Himself (John 15:26, 16:13).
6. Personal pronouns are used when referring to the Holy Spirit (John 14:16–17, John 16:7–15). "Comforter" in John 14:16 is "parakletos" which means "One who comes alongside of to help." The Holy Spirit is always with us, ready to help when we ask Him to.

C. Personal acts are ascribed to the Holy Spirit.

1. Acts 13:2—The Holy Spirit speaks.
2. Romans 8:26—The Holy Spirit intercedes for us.
3. I John 2:20–27; John 14:26—He teaches us.
4. Acts 16:6–7—The Holy Spirit guides Paul, sometimes forbidding things.
5. Genesis 6:3—The Spirit strives with man.

D. The Holy Spirit can receive treatment as a person.

1. Ephesians 4:30—He can be grieved by us.
2. Hebrews 10:29—We can insult Him.
3. Acts 5:3—He can be lied to.
4. Matthew 12:31–32—He can be blasphemed.

E. The Holy Spirit is identified with the Father and the Son as a person.

1. Matthew 28:19—He is named with the Father and Son in baptism.
2. 2 Corinthians 13:14—He is named with the Father and Son in benediction.
3. Acts 15:28—He is identified with the believers as a person.

CHAPTER 2
THE DEITY OF THE HOLY SPIRIT

I. The Trinity in the Shema

A. The Shema, the cornerstone of Judaism, is found in Deuteronomy 6:4.

1. The Hebrew word for *God* in the plural, "Elohim," is used here again.
2. The Hebrew word for *one* is "echad" which is a compound unity, rather than the word "yacheed" which is an absolute one.

II. Attributes of God in the Holy Spirit.

A. God is eternal. Hebrews 9:14 speaks of "the eternal Spirit."

B. God is omniscient (Acts 15:18). Paul in 1 Corinthians 2:10–11 says the things of God are known only by the Spirit.

C. God is omnipresent. In Psalm 139:7, David says the Spirit is everywhere.

D. God is omnipotent. In Luke 1:35, the angel speaks of the Holy Spirit as the power of the Highest.

III. Works of God in the Holy Spirit

A. The Spirit was active in creation.

 1. In Genesis 1:1 the plural word for *God,* "Elohim", indicates that the Trinity worked together.
 2. Genesis 1:2 speaks of the Spirit moving on the face of the waters.
 3. Genesis 1:26 gives us a glimpse of the Trinity working in harmony to create man. "Let Us make man in Our image."
 4. Psalm 104:30 also speaks of the Spirit's part in creation.

B. The Spirit gives life.

 1. In 2 Corinthians 3:6, Paul says the letter of the law kills, but the Spirit gives life.
 2. In John 6:63, Jesus also says that the Spirit makes us alive.
 3. Romans 8:10.

C. The Holy Spirit inspired the Bible. 2 Peter 1:21 declares that "holy men of God spake as they were moved by the Holy Ghost."

D. The Holy Spirit works with the Father and the Son. 1 Corinthians 12:4–6 speaks of the Father, Son and Holy Spirit in the ministries of the church.

IV. Scriptures Relating God and the Holy Spirit

A. There are some Scriptures in the Old Testament that refer to God. In the New Testament the same Scriptures are ascribed to the Holy Spirit, which means they are one God.

 1. Isaiah 6:8–10 refers to God speaking. Acts 28:25–27 quotes the same verse, but says the Holy Spirit said it.

2. In Jeremiah 31:31–33, God made a covenant. In Hebrews 10:15–17, it says the Holy Spirit made the covenant.
3. Psalm 95:7–11 speaks of hearing God's voice. Hebrews 3:7–9 refers to the Holy Spirit speaking there.

B. There are some Scriptures that refer to the Holy Spirit as God.

1. Acts 5:1–11 tells the story of Ananias and Sapphira who "lied to the Holy Ghost." Peter also says, "Thou hast not lied unto men, but unto God." Peter equated the Holy Spirit with God.
2. In 2 Corinthians 3:17–18, Paul speaks of the Lord as the Spirit and makes a direct association of One with the Other.

V. God Deals With Us By the Holy Spirit

A. We deal with God through Jesus (John 14:13 and Hebrews 4:16). God deals with us through the Holy Spirit (Romans 8:16).

B. When we exist on the fleshly level, we are ruled by our bodies, and our souls and spirits are in second and third place. When we are born again, our spirits are moved to the dominant position and the Holy Spirit takes control. He helps us to conform to the image of Christ.

CHAPTER 3
THE WORK OF THE HOLY SPIRIT
IN THE LIFE OF THE BELIEVER

I. The Holy Spirit as Helper

The Holy Spirit is a helper Who comes alongside us to guide us in our Christian walk (John 14:16).

II. The Holy Spirit as Teacher

The Holy Spirit is our Teacher (John 14.26, 1 John 2:27, 1 Corinthians 2:13,14).

A. When we are born again, we enter the dimension of the Spirit. In this dimension, we can be taught by Him to understand the things of God that are beyond the reach of our experience or intellect (2 Corinthians 4:18).

B. The Holy Spirit brings the Scriptures that we have read or heard to our remembrance (John 14:26). It is so good to have the right Scripture come to mind when we need it.

III. The Holy Spirit as Guide
The Holy Spirit will guide us into all truth (John 16:12–13).

   A. He will give us the discernment to judge between true and false teachings.

   B. If we will open our hearts and read the Bible with the Spirit as our guide, we will not stray from the truth and we will have all we need to live the Christian life (2 Peter 1:3).

IV. The Holy Spirit in Prophecy
The Holy Spirit will show us things to come (John 16:13). The Spirit will help us to understand the prophecies in the books of Daniel and Revelation and Ezekiel. Since we are living in the last days, these prophecies are becoming more clear each day.

CHAPTER 4
THE POWER OF THE HOLY SPIRIT IN THE LIFE OF THE BELIEVER

I. The Promise of the Spirit

   A. Acts 1:4–5 contains the promise by the Father to give the Holy Spirit to the believers.

   B. In Joel 2:28, the Father said that in the last days He would pour out His Spirit upon all flesh.

II. The Power of the Spirit

   A. In Acts 1:8, we learn that the Holy Spirit gives us the power to live the Christian life as a witness for God.

   1. It is impossible to live the Christian life without the power of the Spirit within us (Romans 7:15–25, Galatians 5:17–18, Matthew 26:41).
   2. Jesus Christ is our example of the witness that we should be (John 14:8–9).
   3. The word *power* in Greek is "dunamis" from which we derive the English word "dynamic."
   4. The true witness lives his faith.

B. Before Peter received the power of the Holy Spirit, he was afraid to be identified with Jesus (Mark 14:53–72) even though he wanted to (Mark 14:27–31). After he received the power, he witnessed boldly to the same group of people who had tried Jesus (Acts 4:5–23), even telling them that there was no salvation apart from Christ. Then when Peter went back to the Christians, they prayed for greater boldness (v. 23–31).

C. We must allow the Holy Spirit to change us within, rather than trying to change the outside of ourselves and then hoping we will change within (Romans 8). As we yield each area of our lives to the Spirit, He conforms us into the image of Christ.

CHAPTER 5
THE CONFORMING WORK OF THE HOLY SPIRIT

I. The Standard of Righteousness

A. In Matthew 5:20, Jesus told the disciples that they had to be more righteous than the scribes and Pharisees, who rigidly followed the law, if they wanted to enter the kingdom of heaven.

B. In Matthew 5:21–47, Jesus gave illustrations of how the law should be kept. The Pharisees practiced an outward righteousness that conformed to the law, but Jesus said the law required inward purity also.

C. In the last verse of Matthew 5, Jesus told them to be perfect even as the heavenly Father is perfect.

II. Salvation Through Jesus Christ

A. Since we cannot reach the standard of righteousness that God requires, He has given us another way to come to Him. In John 6:28–29, when the people asked Jesus what they should do in order to do the works of God, He told them to "believe on Him Whom He hath sent."

B. When we invite Christ into our lives, the Spirit of God also comes in and begins to work within us to make us more like Christ (2 Corinthians 5:17).

C. Jesus is the example of what God intended man to be when He created him (Genesis 1:26). In John 8:29, Jesus said that He always did the things that pleased the Father, and in Matthew 3:17 God said of Jesus, "This is my beloved Son, in Whom I am well pleased."

III. The Spirit Conforms Us to the Image of Christ

A. God's Spirit works in us to change us into the likeness of Christ (Ephesians 4:13).

B. God's predestined purpose for us was to conform us into the image of His Son (Romans 8:29).

C. When we see the divine ideal for man in Jesus Christ, the Holy Spirit changes us from glory to glory into that same image (2 Corinthians 3:18). We have to see Christ with an open or "unveiled" face, a face that is not blinded to the truth.

D. We can only see Christ in the Word, and we need the Spirit to make the Word alive to our hearts (2 Peter 1:4).

IV. We Become Sons of God Through Christ

A. We become sons of God, not through any righteousness of our own, but by our faith in Jesus Christ (John 1:12, Romans 8:16–17).

B. As we become more like Christ, our problems arise from living as redeemed spirits in unredeemed bodies. We desire to be delivered from these bodies of flesh so that we can enjoy the full, rich, overflowing life in the spirit (1 John 3:2, 2 Corinthians 5:4, Romans 8:22, 23).

C. As the Holy Spirit continues to work in us, we find that our joy is in growing continually more conformed to the image of Christ. "I shall be satisfied when I awake, with Thy likeness" (Psalm 17:15).

CHAPTER 6
THE FRUIT OF THE SPIRIT

I. The Holy Spirit Makes God's Agape Love Available to Us

A. The mark of the Christian is the agape love flowing through him (John 13:35).

B. "Agape" love is the deep, spiritual, giving, godly love that is far above the "eros" (physical love) or the "phileo" (brotherly, companionship love). It is supernatural love.

II. Agape Love Described

A. 1 Corinthians 13 is a beautiful description of agape love.

1. Paul begins his description of agape by giving it the supremacy over other spiritual gifts (v.1–2).
2. Agape is also more important than sacrificing our possessions or our bodies (v. 3).
3. Agape love receives abuse again and again and at the end it is still kind (v. 4).
4. "Seeketh not it's own" means that love does not insist on having its own way (v. 5).
5. The word "easily" was inserted by the translators. Love is not provoked (v. 5).

III. God is the Source of Agape Love

A. When agape love flows through us, we know that we have passed from death into life (1 John 3:14).

B. We cannot generate agape love when we need it. When we find ourselves lacking in love, we need to ask God to fill our hearts with agape by His Holy Spirit.

C. Our flesh battles with the Spirit when we want to do the right thing (Galatians 5:17).

IV. The Fruit of the Spirit is Agape

A. In Galatians 5:19–23 the works of the flesh are contrasted with the fruit of the Spirit.

The realm of works is the realm of the flesh. Fruit is God's method; it is the natural consequence of relationship.

B. As we abide in Christ, we bear fruit. When we bear fruit, the Father washes and cleanses us so that we will continue to bear. If we do not abide in Christ, we will not be able to produce fruit (John 15:1–8).

C. While the gifts of the Spirit are valuable and necessary, Paul recommends the fruit of the Spirit as "a more excellent way" (1 Corinthians 12:31).

D. "But the fruit of the Spirit is love (agape)" (Galatians 5:22). There is one fruit of the Spirit followed by eight adjectives that define the supernatural love of God.
   1. Joy is love's consciousness. When we love, we are so filled with joy that even normally miserable tasks are pleasurable.
   2. Peace is more than the cessation of hostilities. Love that wishes no ill is the basis for true peace.
   3. Longsuffering is the characteristic of love that makes us kind after being continually mistreated, without keeping track of the offenses.
   4. Love is gentle, not harsh or abrasive.
   5. Love is the only positive motive for goodness. Some people are "good" because they fear the consequences of doing something wrong, but that is not true goodness.
   6. The faith mentioned in this verse is not the gift of the Spirit listed in 1 Corinthians 12:9 but is a loving trust in people.
   7. Meekness does not vaunt itself and does not seek praise and honor.
   8. Temperance is moderation.

E. These characteristics of agape love are the result of the Holy Spirit's work in our lives.

CHAPTER 7
THE HOLY SPIRIT AS BIBLE EXPOSITOR

I. Instruction of the Holy Spirit

The Holy Spirit makes the things of God and the Word of God clear to us (1 Corinthians 2:10).

A. The natural man cannot understand the things of God because he does not have the Holy Spirit to teach him (1 Corinthians 2:14).

B. The Spirit has revealed unto us the things God has prepared for us because we love Him (1 Corinthians 2:9–10). These are things that God has for His people now, not heavenly things.

C. "For what man knoweth the things of a man, save the spirit of man which is in him?" We may deceive other people because only we know what is really in our hearts. "Even so the things of God knoweth no man, but the Spirit of God" (1 Corinthians 2:11). There are some aspects of God that man cannot understand, and only the Spirit knows them.

D. Many people try to discover what the Bible is all about by approaching it with their human intellect. They cannot understand spiritual things without the Holy Spirit to open their minds (1 Corinthians 2:12–14), so it appears foolish to them.

II. The Holy Spirit: Our Teacher and Guide in Spiritual Things

A. Jesus promised that the Holy Spirit would be our teacher (John 14:26). When we sit down to read the Bible, we should always begin by asking the Holy Spirit to open our minds and hearts to receive and understand what we are reading (1 John 2:27).

B. The Word of God is our spiritual food and we cannot grow as Christians without it.

C. It is important that we read the Bible to plant the Scriptures in our minds for the Holy Spirit to bring them to our remembrance when we need them (John 14:26, Psalm 119:11).

D. The Holy Spirit guides us into the truth of God and shows us the things that are going to happen so that we are prepared (John 16:13, 1 Thessalonians 5:4).

CHAPTER 8
THE HOLY SPIRIT IN THE WORLD

I. Jesus Promised To Send the Holy Spirit

   A. When Jesus ministered here on earth, He was restricted to being in one place at a time. The Holy Spirit can be everywhere at once because He is not limited by a body (John 16:7).

   B. Since the Word was to go out to all parts of the earth, Jesus could minister to the church more effectively by the Holy Spirit.

II. The Work of the Holy Spirit Within the World

   A. Jesus said that the Holy Spirit would reprove the world of sin because people do not believe in Him (John 16:8–9). The only sin that condemns a man is the continual rejection of Jesus Christ as Lord and Savior (John 3:17–18). This sin is also the unpardonable sin of blasphemy against the Holy Spirit because the Holy Spirit convicts us of sin.

   B. The Holy Spirit reproves the world of righteousness because Jesus ascended into heaven (John 16:8–10). When God received Jesus up into heaven, He was setting the standard of righteousness a man would have to meet to be acceptable to God.

   C. The Holy Spirit reproves the world of judgment because the prince of this world (Satan) is judged (John 16:8–11).

      1. When Jesus went to the cross and died in our place, Satan lost his power over us to force us to do those things that are contrary to God's righteousness (Colossians 2:14–15).

         a. Our old nature, which was subject to sin and to Satan, was put to death at the cross of Christ (Romans 6:6).

         b. What does it mean when we sin? It means that we have not appropriated what God has made available to us through the power of Christ and the Holy Spirit. We need to consciously yield to the power of the Spirit and to that victory of Christ over Satan.

c. Any power that Satan exerts in our lives today is usurped because he has no authority over us and no right to try to control us. If we demand in the name of Jesus Christ that Satan go, then he must.

   d. When we pray to ask God for His help in removing Satan from our lives, we should be very specific, because Satan is so stubborn that he won't want to relinquish any foothold that he does not have to. Also, once he is driven out, he will launch a counter-attack to win the area back, so remember to hold onto what you take through the power of the Holy Spirit by continual prayer.

CHAPTER 9
THE WORK OF THE HOLY SPIRIT IN THE LAST DAYS

I. The Hindering Force of the Holy Spirit

A. The Bible says that in the last days there will be "distress of nations, with perplexity" (Luke 21:25). The word translated "perplexity" also means "no way out." The nations will have problems that they cannot solve.

B. 2 Thessalonians 2:1–12 reveals the work of the Holy Spirit in the last days.

   1. In verse 3 the "falling away" refers to the departure of the church.

      a. This will be the time when Jesus Christ will come for His church. He will not return to earth at this time, but we will be caught up ("snatched up" in Greek) to meet Him in the air.

      b. His second coming will occur seven years later when He returns to earth with His church to establish His kingdom (Colossians 3:4, Jude 14, Revelation 19:14).

   2. The "son of perdition" is the Antichrist, who will cause his image to be set up in the temple in Jerusalem (v. 4). This is the "abomination of desolation" prophesied in Daniel 9:27, 11:31, 12:11, and in Matthew 24:15.

   3. Verse 6 refers to the power of the Holy Spirit in withholding or hindering Satan from presenting the Antichrist to a world that has been conditioned to accept him.

a. The economy will stabilize when the Antichrist introduces his identification number system to use in buying and selling (Revelation 13:14–17). People are using credit cards for more and more purchases, so they are used to using a number in business transactions.
   b. There is no charismatic, strong political leader on the scene right now. People have lost confidence in their political systems and are looking for a man with the answers (Daniel 9:26–27—"Week" refers to 7 years here).
   c. People are tired of the troubled Mideast situation and of the continual wars around the world. They will hail the Antichrist as a man of peace because his peace plan will work for 3 1/2 years.
4. The spirit of Antichrist is already at work in the world (v. 7 and 1 John 4:3). Satan would like to put this master deceiver in power now (v. 8–12), but the Holy Spirit is holding him back until He takes the church to heaven (v. 6).
   a. In Revelation 4:1, the rapture of the church occurs and the next big event on earth is the appearance of the Antichrist riding a white horse (symbolizing his false righteousness) and leading the people to believe that he has brought a lasting peace (Revelation 6:2).
5. As Christians, we should not be concerned with looking for the Antichrist, but we should be looking for the glorious appearance of Jesus Christ (Luke 21:28, Matthew 25:1–13, Romans 13:11).

CHAPTER 10
THE SEAL OF THE HOLY SPIRIT

I. The Blessing of the Child of God

A. In Ephesians 1:1–14, Paul lists the wonderful blessings we have as children of God. We are blessed by being chosen, predestined, accepted, redeemed, and forgiven. God also makes His will known to us and gives an inheritance to us.

1. In verse 13, Paul talks about the Christian being sealed "with that Holy Spirit of promise." First we must hear the gospel (Romans 10:14), become aware that our sins separate us from God (Isaiah 59:1–2), then believe in Christ as God's plan for our salvation (John 3:16). After we believe, we are sealed by the Holy Spirit.
   a. In the days when the Bible was written, the seal was used primarily as a stamp of ownership. Roman merchants would travel to Ephesus to choose their goods, stamp them with their signet rings, and then return home. When their goods arrived at the port near Rome, the merchants claimed their merchandise that they had sealed.
   b. Once we believe, God claims us as His possessions. The seal of God's ownership is the Holy Spirit indwelling our lives.

B. 2 Corinthians 1:22 also deals with the seal of the Holy Spirit. Speaking of God, Paul says, "Who hath also sealed us and given the earnest of the Spirit in our hearts." The "earnest" here means a deposit or down payment. The Holy Spirit is not only the seal of God's ownership, but He is the down payment until He redeems us as His purchased possession.

C. In Ephesians 4:30, we are told, "And grieve not the Holy Spirit of God whereby ye are sealed unto the day of redemption." Ephesians 1:14 also speaks of the Christian being sealed "until the redemption." God declares His intention of completing our redemption by giving the Holy Spirit to us. Our redemption will not be complete until we are freed from our bodies.
   1. Paul speaks of the Christian being "burdened" with a body (2 Corinthians 5:4) and of all creation groaning, waiting for the redemption of our bodies (Romans 8:22–23).
   2. Paul also speaks of the new bodies God will give to us as a "building of God, a house not made with hands, eternal in the heavens" (2 Corinthians 5:1), while he refers to our present bodies as tents (tabernacles). We think of tents as temporary dwellings while a house is permanent. Our redemption by God will include new heavenly bodies that will not be subject to the pain, fatigue, or temptations of the flesh.

3. In Revelation 5, John describes the scene in heaven as Jesus completes the redemption. Jesus purchased the earth with His death on the cross and then sealed all those who accepted salvation through Him. Now we are waiting for God to finish His work of redemption in us, and it will take place very soon. Hallelujah!

CHAPTER 11
THE WORK OF THE HOLY SPIRIT IN THE CHURCH

I. The Purpose of the Gifts of the Spirit

   A. In 1 Corinthians 12, Paul discusses the proper balance of the use of the gifts of the Spirit within the church.

      1. In verse 1, the word "gifts" was added by the translators. Paul used the word "pneumatikos" which means "spirituals." Paul had been dealing with carnal problems earlier in his epistle, and now he was moving into the subject of spiritual things—"Now concerning spirituals, brethren, I would not have you ignorant."
      2. In verse 7, Paul tells the Corinthians that "the manifestation of the Spirit is given to every man to profit withal." God does not give the gifts of the Spirit to us so that we can retreat from others to enjoy the blessings of God. Instead, the gifts and manifestations of the Spirit are to benefit the whole church. God does not give the gifts to exalt individuals, He gives them to exalt Jesus Christ.

         a. The one exception to this rule about gifts is the gift of tongues. The gift of tongues is given to build up the believer. Paul spoke of the abundant use of tongues in his own prayer life but he said, "He that speaketh in an unknown tongue edifieth himself."

II. The Church As the Body of Christ

   A. Just as there are diversities of gifts and diversities of operations (1 Corinthians 12:4–6), so there are different parts and functions in the body. Paul often makes the analogy that the body of Christ is like the human body (1 Corinthians 12:12–31, Ephesians 4:15–16 Romans 12:4–5).

1. When we see the church as a body, we should see Christ as the head. He should be in charge, directing the body. The Holy Spirit is the nervous system of the body, taking the messages from Jesus to the various parts of the body and then coordinating them for smooth movement.
2. Every part of the body has a vital function to perform. We have to function in that place in the body where God has put us without striving or feeling jealous of those put in other places. If our lives don't seem to be flowing, we should check to see that we are involved in Spirit-directed endeavors rather than in activities that we have chosen for ourselves.
3. The Spirit is sovereign in the bestowing of spiritual gifts (1 Corinthians 12:31); the Holy Spirit decides what my gift in the body shall be.
4. The body needs all of its parts to function properly. We need to gather together for worship, fellowship, and ministry.
5. We should be sensitive to each other, suffering with another member when he suffers, and rejoicing sincerely with another member when he is exalted (1 Corinthians 12:26; Romans 6:13).

III. The Ministry Gifts Within the Body

A. In Ephesians 4, Paul discusses the ministry gifts within the body.

1. In verse 12, Paul says the purpose of the ministry gifts is to perfect the saints and to edify (build up) the body of Christ.
2. In verse 13, we read that the Holy Spirit is working in the body to bring us to "the measure of the stature of the fullness of Christ."
3. In verses 14–16, Paul again makes the point that the Holy Spirit uses the gifts to build up the body of Christ.

IV. How to Receive the Gifts of the Spirit

A. In Romans 12, Paul explains how we receive the gifts of the Spirit, how we can be used of God, and how we can find our place in the body.

1. In verses 1 and 2, Paul says that we can know God's perfect will for our lives by presenting our bodies to Him "holy and acceptable" and as "a living sacrifice."

a. We cannot allow ourselves to be conformed to worldly patterns, we must be transformed to godliness by "renewing our minds," that is, by seeking God and waiting on Him for direction.
  2. In verse 3, Paul prefaces his remarks about spiritual gifts with a warning that we not think too highly of ourselves. One of the greatest dangers in the use of the spiritual gifts is pride. We need to constantly be aware that God is demonstrating His grace when He uses us, because we are worthless sinners without Him.

CHAPTER 12
THE FLOWING OF THE SPIRIT
IN THE CHURCH

I. Instruments of the Holy Spirit

God is looking for instruments through which He might do the work that He desires to do in the world (2 Chronicles 16:9). If our hearts and lives are in harmony with the purposes of God, He will use us as channels for His love, power and Spirit to flow to the needy world. The Holy Spirit was given to help us to become aligned with God's purpose and plan.

II. The Flowing of the Spirit

  A. When we received salvation we also received the Holy Spirit to dwell within us, but there is a deeper relationship we can experience.
   1. In John 7:37–39, John tells of Jesus promising that those who drink of the water that He gives will have torrents of water gushing from them. John explains that Jesus was speaking of the Holy Spirit. We can have the Spirit flowing from our lives in torrents.
   2. In Acts 8:15–17, Peter and John went to Samaria to pray that the believers would receive the Holy Spirit "for as yet He was fallen upon (the epi experience) none of them." The epi experience produces the overflowing of the Holy Spirit within our lives.
   3. In Acts 19:1–6, Paul went to Ephesus and prayed that the believers there would receive the Holy Spirit.

III. The Manifestations of the Holy Spirit

  A. In 1 Corinthians 12:31, Paul commands us to earnestly desire the "best gifts." What are the best gifts?

1. If you need to communicate to God the praise and the love that is deep within your heart, the best gift for that circumstance is tongues (1 Corinthians 14:14).
2. If someone is sick, the best gift for that situation is the gift of healing.
3. If someone is blind, the gift of miracles would probably be best.
4. If we are open to God and walking in the Spirit, He can manifest any of the gifts through us. Usually we are given a particular gift, though.

B. In 1 Corinthians 12:8–12, Paul gives a partial list of the gifts of the Spirit. All these gifts are exercised through faith, as Paul mentions in Romans 12:6 concerning the gift of prophecy.

  1. There is a difference between the word of wisdom and the word of knowledge. Knowledge is the assimilation of facts; wisdom is the proper application of knowledge.

     a. When Stephen stood before the council, the Holy Spirit gave him the word of wisdom (Acts 7).
     b. When Paul stood before the council, the Holy Spirit gave him the word of wisdom also (Acts 23).
     c. When the chief priests and elders tried to trap Jesus with tricky questions, He had the word of wisdom in operation when He answered (Luke 20:21–26, Matthew 21:23–27).
     d. James was given the word of wisdom when the church had to settle the Gentile issue (Acts 15:13–21).
     e. One of the big problems of the Christian life is determining whether something has come from our own minds or as inspiration from God. Peter had this problem when he declared that Jesus was God's Son by the inspiration of the Spirit, and then rebuked Jesus by thoughts from Satan (Matthew 16:13–23). To help us with this problem, God has given the gift of the discerning of spirits (v. 10).

CHAPTER 13
THE WORD OF KNOWLEDGE

I. The Manifestations of the Word of Knowledge

A. The Holy Spirit gives spiritual gifts to us according to His will. Though He may give two people the same gift, the gift may operate differently in them (diversities of operations—1 Corinthians 12:6).

B. Jesus often manifested the gift of the word of knowledge (Colossians 2:3).

   1. When Nathaniel was brought to Jesus, the Lord told him what he had been doing earlier (John 1:45–51).
   2. Jesus sent His disciples into town and told them how it would be when they were there (Mark 11:1–7, Luke 22:7–13).
   3. Jesus told Peter to catch a fish, open its mouth and remove a coin, and pay the tax man (Matthew 17:24–27).

C. Elisha exercised the word of knowledge more fully than most of the Old Testament prophets.

   1. He warned the king of Israel of the Syrian king's plans (2 Kings 6:8–12).
   2. He told Naaman he would be healed if he would wash in the Jordan River seven times (2 Kings 5:19).
   3. He told his servant Gehazi what was in Gehazi's mind (2 Kings 5:20–27).
   4. He told the Shunammite woman that she would have a son the next year (2 Kings 4:16–17).
   5. When the Shunammite woman's son died, the Lord did not reveal it to Elisha, and Elisha was surprised because he was so accustomed to knowing what was happening (2 Kings 4:27).
      a. We know from this that the gifts of God are totally His to control and not something we can operate of our own volition.

D. Paul the apostle exercised the gift of knowledge.

   1. When Paul went to Rome by ship, he warned the men on board that they would lose the ship (Acts 27:10).
   2. Later, Paul told them that no one on board would die (Acts 27:23–26) but that they would be cast up on an island.

E. We need to have times for meditation when we consciously seek to hear God's voice to have the word of knowledge, though sometimes God gives it to us when we are in the midst of other things.

CHAPTER 14
THE GIFT OF DISCERNING OF SPIRITS

I. Discerning of Spirits

A. In Revelation 2:2, Jesus commended the church at Ephesus because they could discern spirits. They recognized the false apostles and rejected their teaching.

B. False prophets or teachers often say mostly true things. We must listen very carefully because their lies are subtle and the errors they teach are damning.

C. People are often taken in by false prophets because they don't listen carefully. They are lulled by the truth in the message and do not catch the lies.

D. Another reason people are led astray by false teaching is that they really don't know God's Word. They haven't grounded their faith in the Bible by careful study.

E. There are two ways to test for a false prophet.
   1. Listen to his testimony.
   2. See if he puts a strong emphasis on money. (When God guides, God provides).

CHAPTER 15
THE GIFT OF FAITH

I. Our Faith Comes From God

A. Jesus commanded us to "have faith in God" (Mark 11:22), and He gave us the capacity to fulfill His command (Romans 12:3, Hebrews 12:2).

B. Hebrews 11 deals with faith from God.
   1. Faith is believing what we cannot see (v. 1).
   2. When we come to God, we must believe two things: (1) that He is, and (2) that He rewards those who seek Him (v. 6).
   3. Faith helps us to do the impossible (v. 33–36).

II. Limitless Faith

A. If we know God, we will not limit His work in our lives. His Word will give us the proper concept of Him (Romans 4:21).

B. Our faith in God is not blind. The man of faith often sees more than others can see (2 Kings 6:15–17; Hebrews 11:27).

C. There is "saving faith" (Ephesians 2:8) and "active faith" (Exodus 14:15; Joshua 3, Joshua 6). The men of active faith see more in the promise of God to deliver them than in the power of the enemy to destroy them. This faith is more than just believing–it is stepping out.

III. The Gift of Faith

A. The gift of faith must be used in love (1 Corinthians 13:2).

B. All the gifts of the Spirit are received and exercised by faith (Romans 12:6).

C. Sometimes several gifts of the Spirit are in operation at the same time, but the Spirit makes everything harmonious and never interrupts Himself (Acts 14:8–11, Acts 20:9–12, Acts 3:1–8).

D. Peter said that faith in Jesus and the faith by Jesus healed a man (Acts 3:16).

E. When we exercise our faith, we receive more faith.

F. Satan waits at the foot of every spiritual mountain to destroy our faith (Matthew 17:1–2).

G. Our faith is tested when we don't see immediate results after we have stepped out in faith. Sometimes there is a time interval before God makes His move, and we must wait for Him with faith and patience (Hebrews 11:1, 10:36, 6:12, James 1:3).

CHAPTER 16
THE GIFT OF MIRACLES

I. The Nature of Miracles

A. If we cannot believe in God, we cannot believe in miracles (Acts 26:8).

B. A miracle is God operating according to laws higher than the laws of nature that we know and understand. He supersedes the laws we know (Isaiah 55:8; Colossians 2:2–3).

1. There are things we accept today that would have been considered miracles a hundred years ago.
2. When a law of nature is superseded by another law, the law of nature is not negated.

C. The dangers of miracles.

1. It is dangerous to follow after miracles because not all miracles are of God; some are of Satan and meant to deceive (2 Thessalonians 2:9).
2. If we have the gift of miracles operating through us, there is a temptation to use miracles for our own benefit (Luke 4:1–4).
3. There is a danger that we will accept adulation from people for miracles performed through us (Acts 14:8–18).

II. The Gift of Miracles

A. God wants to work miracles in our time just as He did thorugh Moses, Elisha, Jonah, Jesus, Phillip, Paul, and Peter. He will use us if we have been crucified with Christ and are letting Christ live through us (Galatians 2:20).

B. If we have the gift of miracles it does not mean we can work miracles anytime we want to. The Holy Spirit controls this gift.

C. We need to expand the limits of what we think God can do. He can do anything! (Genesis 18:14).

CHAPTER 17
THE GIFT OF HEALING

I. Sickness and Healing

A. Sickness and aging came into the world with the sin of Adam and Eve. A sick person is not necessarily sick because of sin in his life, but because of sin in the world.

B. Isaiah 53:5–7 speaks prophetically of the beating that Jesus took for our healing. Jesus purchased our salvation at the cross and our healing at the whipping post.

C. God promised to heal us (Exodus 15:26).

D. Jesus' ministry was full of healings (Acts 10:38). He sent His disciples out to heal the people in His name and healing is a mark of the believer (Matthew 10:1; Mark 16:15–18).

E. Some say that miracles and healings ended for the church with the time of the apostles, but A. Gordon in his book, *The Ministry of Healing,* reports that healings have taken place throughout the history of the church.

II. The Gift of Healing

A. If we are healed, we have received the gift of healing. Sometimes the gift of healing operates through us to heal someone else.

B. There are diversities in the operation of the gift of healing. The gift does not work the same through everyone.

C. We do not have to have the gift of healing to pray for someone to be healed. The believers should pray for one another (James 5:14).

D. During the communion service, we are to appropriate the healing that Jesus purchased for us when He allowed His body to be broken (Luke 22:19) by the beating (1 Corinthians 11:30).

CHAPTER 18
THE GIFT OF TONGUES

I. About the Gift of Tongues

A. Jesus said that speaking in tongues would be a sign of a believer (Mark 16:17).

B. Acts 2 contains an account of how the gift of tongues was given to the believers. "As the Spirit gave them utterance" could also be translated "as the Spirit prompted their speech" or "as the Spirit gave them ability to speak" (v. 4). The multitude that gathered heard the believers speaking in several different dialects.

C. Language is an agreement between people that certain sounds have certain meanings.

II. Uses of the Gift of Tongues

A. The gift of tongues allows us by the Spirit to express ourselves to God without funneling our feelings through our intellect. When words cannot express what we feel, we use a spiritual language that is beyond the limits of our understanding, so our prayer life is more satisfying (1 Corinthians 14:4).

B. Paul taught that the best use of the gift of tongues is in our private devotions rather than in public worship (1 Corinthians 14).

   1. The purpose of the gift of tongues is to communicate with God.
   2. Although some churches allow what they call "messages in tongues" to be delivered during public services, actually these utterances are not "messages" at all, because tongues are directed to God.
   3. Many times the "interpretation" that follows a "message in tongues" is really a prophecy, because it is spoken from God to the church. An interpretation of tongues will be prayer to God (Acts 2:11).
   4. Paul indicated that we can control the gift of tongues. The Spirit does not compel someone to interrupt a service with tongues. We can speak to God quietly within ourselves if we feel the Spirit moving (1 Corinthians 14:28, 33).
   5. When a person shouts, uses a shrill tone, or sustains sounds, that is not the Spirit speaking but the person reacting to Him. We can whisper in tongues if we choose to.

C. The Spirit helps us in our prayer life when we do not know how to pray for a situation (Romans 8:26, 27).

   1. If we are unaware of needs or unsure of God's will in a matter that needs prayer, we can sometimes ask Him to do something that is in direct opposition to His will. Our prayer in the Spirit is always according to the will of God.
   2. When we pray in the Spirit, we pray unhindered by our flesh, so selfishness and other sinful attitudes are eliminated from our prayer (James 4:2–3).

D. If a person does not want to use the gift of tongues in his prayer life, he has probably magnified his intellect to the point that he will not say anything that his intellect cannot grasp. Therefore, his prayer life is limited to English, (or in the language he is most fluent in) and he misses a rich dimension in his prayer life.

CHAPTER 19
THE GIFT OF TONGUES AND INTERPRETATION

I. Tongues and the Believer

A. The gift of tongues is not the only evidence of the filling of the Holy Spirit.

B. In 1 Corinthians 14, there seems to be an inconsistency between v. 22 and vs. 23–24. J. B. Phillips believes the copyists made an error in v. 22 and meant to say that tongues are not for a sign to believers and that prophecy is. Perhaps Paul meant that tongues serve as an evidence to a person that he has been filled with the Spirit, since some people have trouble believing that God will fill them if they simply ask Him to.

C. Some people feel that the gift of tongues was for the early church but not for today.

   1. They use 1 Corinthians 13:8 as the basis for their belief. However, prophecies have not failed and knowledge has increased, rather than vanished.
   2. They say v. 10, "that which is perfect," refers to the Bible and that since we have the complete Scriptures, tongues are unnecessary. However, tongues were never used as a teaching tool like the Bible is. We believe "that which is perfect" refers to Jesus and His second coming and that prophecy and tongues are valid gifts until then.

II. The Interpretation of Tongues

A. If we speak in tongues in a group of believers, we need to pray for the interpretation (1 Corinthians 14:13). Otherwise, we are edified but the others are not (v. 16–19).

B. An interpretation of tongues is usually the expression of thoughts that are given to us by the Spirit.

C. Interpretations of tongues will be prayers offered to God. If someone gives an "interpretation" addressed to the church, then it is actually a prophecy, not an interpretation of tongues.

CHAPTER 20
THE GIFT OF PROPHECY

I. Prophecy in the Bible

A. The Old Testament prophets were used by God to warn the nation of forthcoming judgment and to promise the Kingdom Age. They were foretelling future events.

B. New Testament prophets usually were "forthtelling" God's message to the church. The exception is Agabus who foretold a drought (Acts 11:27–28) and Paul's imprisonment (Acts 21:10–14).

II. The Gift of Prophecy

A. The gift of prophecy has greater value in the church than the gift of tongues (1 Corinthians 14:2–5).

B. The purposes of the gift of prophecy.
   1. Jesus Christ is edified (built up) in us by the encouragement and reassurance in prophecies.
   2. The church is exhorted to Christian activity to trust, pray, praise, step out in faith in prophecies. Praise is especially important for the church to practice (Psalm 22:3).

C. It takes faith for any spiritual gifts to operate in us because we must cooperate with divine power, rather than a material power. He does not totally take us over, so we must consciously take part (1 Corinthians 14:32).

D. When God speaks to us in prophecy, His Spirit speaks to our spirit, not to our intellect (Romans 8:16).

E. When the Spirit told the church to send our missionaries, He probably spoke through the prophets in the church (Acts 13:1–2).

III. How To Judge Prophecy

A. Not everything that sounds like prophecy is truly prophecy (1 Corinthians 14:29), so we must judge prophecy to discern truth from error.

1. The basis for judging prophecies:

    a. Is it in harmony with the written Word of God (Galatians 1:8)?

    b. Does it come to pass (Deuteronomy 18:20–22)? It must be 100% accurate (1 John 4:1–6).

    c. What does it teach about Jesus Christ and salvation?

IV. Speaking a Prophecy

A. Prophecy usually comes to us as a thought or a thought pattern. Sometimes only one sentence comes until we have spoken it, and then the rest of the prophecy flows forth. We need to take the first step by faith.

B. God reveals His will and plans for us through prophecy, so it is a useful gift in the church.

CHAPTER 21
GIFT OF HELPS

In 1 Corinthians 12:28, the ministries are listed and then the gifts that help us to fulfill those ministries. God equips us for the ministry He calls us to.

The gift of helps is what Christianity is all about. It takes thought and consideration to perform this ministry. The Spirit makes us sensitive and attuned to one another (1 Corinthians 12:26).

A. The gifts of helps are a witness to others of Christ in us. These gifts are practical evidence of love. They should be done with cheerfulness (hilarity) and as unto the Lord (Romans 12:8, Colossians 3:17).

B. We should exercise the ministry of helps so that we are not seeking praise from others for ourselves. God should receive the glory from what we do.

C. We need to be satisfied with where God places us in the body and fulfill our ministry joyfully as unto Him.

CHAPTER 22
GIFT OF GOVERNMENTS

I. Laboring for the Lord

A. Our labor for the Lord is not in vain, for He will reward us for the work that we do, rather than its results (1 Corinthians 15:58).

B. Giving ourselves to God as a living sacrifice is the smartest thing we can do, because the Christian life is rich and fulfilling, and God rewards us for faithful service at the end.

C. I cannot do the work of God with carnal methods. I must present my body to God for His use and yield to the Holy Spirit's guidance, and my labor will not be in vain.

II. Gift of Government

A. God anoints and enables individuals to help in the administration and government of the church (1 Corinthians 12:28, Romans 12:8 "he that ruleth").

B. In many churches the men on the board are not the most spiritual men in the church. When they strive for power, two things happen to them:
  1. They seek to perpetuate themselves in power.
  2. They seek to extend their power.

C. We must remember that Jesus is the head of the church. He governs over all and makes the decisions. We are always to be in subservience to Him, even if we are in governing positions.
  1. When we rule, people should know that God is ruling through us.
  2. We should be wary of our flesh because it wants to rule over people.
  3. Spirit-governed leadership constantly inquires of the Lord and is diligent in its duties.

D. There are always areas where government is necessary in the church. In the early church when the apostles needed administrators, they looked for "men of honest report, full of the Holy Ghost and wisdom" (Acts 6:1–6).

E. Natural capacities or education are not as important in church leaders as is a yielded attitude to the Spirit. An uneducated Spirit-filled man can govern better than a man with a doctorate who is not Spirit-filled.

F. We should never shy away from the work God calls us to do (Moses, Jonah, and Jeremiah did for a time) because our ability doesn't count. God just wants people to work through, and He can only use us if we allow Him free access to every part of ourselves.

CHAPTER 23
GIFTS OF TEACHING AND EXHORTATION

The gifts of teaching and exhortation are mentioned in Romans 12:6–8 and in 1 Corinthians 12:11.

I. The Necessity of the Gift of Teaching

A. Often when the gift of teaching is in operation, other gifts are operating with it (word of wisdom, word of knowledge, prophecy).

B. The gift of teaching has not been given the recognition it deserves because many people believe that knowing something makes them teachers.

C. The gift of teaching is not often sought in ministers because it is not as immediately effective as the gift of exhortation. The gift of exhortation is sought, to the neglect of teaching because it excites people and stirs them into activity.

D. Teaching gives us the tools to do the job we have been exhorted to do. There should be a balance in the operation of these gifts (Romans 10:2).

II. The Church and the Gifts of Teaching and Exhortation

A. The growth of a church built on teaching is slow and solid while the growth built on emotion is fast and transient.

B. If the pastor of a church believes that the primary goal of the church is the evangelization of the world, his flock will be fed milky salvation messages week after week. Ephesians 4:8–13 says the purpose of the gifts is for the perfecting of the church for the work of the ministry.

The church exists:
1. For God—His church was purchased with His blood.
2. For itself—The church builds up and perfects the saints until they are in the image of Jesus Christ.
3. To do the work of the Lord.

C. When the church is what God intends for it to be, when love flows and people are being taught and growing, it attracts those outside because they feel the love and see the sincerity of the people.

III. The Study of God's Word

　A. We need to lay the foundation of our relationship with God deep in the rich soil of the Word.

　B. We cannot choose to become teachers because teaching is a gift that God bestows as He deems best, but we should study the Bible diligently in case God does call us into a teaching ministry. If we open ourselves to whatever ministry and gift He has for us and follow the direction He gives to us, we will be able to fill our place in the Body.

CHAPTER 24
THE GIFTS OF GIVING AND MERCY

I. The Ministries in the Body

　A. In Romans 12 and 1 Corinthians 12, Paul compares the church to the human body. The church has often looked uncoordinated with factions pulling it in different directions. The Holy Spirit unifies the body and helps it to coordinate in a smooth movement.

　B. Some ministries in the body receive more attention than others. Paul warns against a pride in our ministry that leads us to draw attention and glory to ourselves (Romans 12:3).

　C. There are some ministries that are as important as the more noticeable gifts but are rarely seen. The gift of giving (Romans 12:8 "he that giveth") is one of these.

　　1. There are some people who are always willing to share their money or their time with those in need. God channels abundant resources into these people because He knows His gifts will not be bottled up but will flow through those with the gift of giving (2 Chronicles 16:9).

　　2. Our giving should be with simplicity rather than with a display (Luke 21:1–4). Unfortunately, the church often encourages the wrong kind of giving and people lose their heavenly reward for what they have given (Matthew 6:1–4).

　　3. We should not give with any strings or attachments. We should not allow the recipient to feel obligated to us.

4. The resources will dwindle if we start to bottle them up or use them for ourselves.

D. Those who are given the gift of mercy are able to build up a member with spiritual needs without making him uncomfortable.

1. Those who have fallen need to know that the door back to God is still open and that He is merciful and forgiving. We should be merciful and forgiving, too.
2. We should be aware that a harsh and condemning attitude is not as effective in dealing with a wayward saint as love is. We should go to the person in meekness and gentleness in an attempt to restore him to fellowship, remembering that we encounter temptations too (Galatians 6:1).

CHAPTER 25
HOW TO RECEIVE YOUR GIFT OF THE SPIRIT

I. Preparation for the Ministry

A. Paul begins his chapter on ministries and gifts with a challenge to present our bodies to God (Romans 12:1). This is the first step we must take to receive our gift.

B. Though the Holy Spirit is sovereign in giving gifts, Paul's command to "covet [desire] earnestly" the best gifts suggests that we don't have to be passive.

1. We should actively seek our gift from the Spirit for our ministry within the body.
2. If we wait upon God, put ourselves in a position to receive from Him, and be available for Him to use, He will begin to use us.
3. We will receive our gift from the Spirit (Galatians 3:2) by faith.

II. Exercising Our Gift

A. Paul reminds Timothy in both his epistles to use the gift he had received "by prophecy, with the laying on of the hands of the presbytery (elders)" (1 Timothy 4:1) and "by the putting on of my hands" (2 Timothy 1:6).

1. It is quite scriptural to have others pray for us to receive our gift.

2. Timothy was apparently reticent or reluctant to use the gift he had received. We need to remember that God will do the work in us; we need only to be willing vessels.

B. We must be careful not to draw attention to ourselves as the vessel God uses. The vessel should not flavor the contents.

1. When Jesus performed miracles, the people glorified God (Luke 5:26 is one of many examples).
2. Paul said, "But I keep under my body (literally: 'I beat myself black and blue') and bring it into subjection" (1 Corinthians 9:27).

C. When God begins to exercise a gift in our lives, Satan is always there to challenge the exercise of the gift.

D. We begin to exercise our gift or ministry within the body by starting where we are in our small circle of fellowship. From there, the Lord may give us bigger things to do. If He doesn't, we shouldn't mind because we should be happy just to be serving Him.

E. God has a specific ministry for each of us. When our hearts are completely open to whatever He may ask us to do, we have taken the first step toward beginning our ministry in the body of Christ.

THE WORD
FOR TODAY
PO Box 8000 Costa Mesa CA 92628
(714) 825-9673 • (800) 272-WORD (9673)
Web site: http://www.twft.com